THE HOME BUSINESS MANUAL

MAKING MONEY FROM YOUR HOME IN THE RECESSION

WRITTEN BY

JOANNA AKINS

Many thanks to my partner and better half Sola, your support is priceless. Thanks to my dad and mum for been there for me always. AK, RJ and Leks you guys are the best brothers in the world.

To my lovely kids this book is dedicated to you.

Thank you Dr Ruth Ibemesim, your careful and excellent editing of this book made it beautiful for all to read.

Table of contents

INTRODUCTION

There is a world of relevant information and opportunities out there for anyone who would like to own a home based business. The world's recession is having a negative effect on many bank accounts and many people have lost their jobs or have had to stop working at their day jobs. I have had a lot of fun researching a list of opportunities available to make some money with very little capital but with lots of hard work. There are many people caught up in similar situations, many people are not able to get an office or a day job and are also not able to run a business in a separate location as well, this becomes extremely frustrating when bills are left unpaid and money is running out. I decided to do a little research on the possibilities of running a home business, and also to find out if it was really possible to make money from the comfort of your home. There is a sense of self worth you get when you have a means of livelihood especially when you are running your own business and making some difference in the life of those around you. A lot of people want to desperately quit the rat race and just be able to have a great work/life balance, and most are wondering where to start from or what to do. My research has shown that there are many opportunities to choose from. These opportunities do not create overnight millionaires but they are genuine methods and ways of creating multiples streams of income. Commitment, hard work and focus are all required to succeed in any home based business as well as research and lots of planning. You will be able to manage your time as you like, and you will be able to work within your own time schedule.

Working from home is not really for everyone, the buzz of the market place keeps some people alive and they cannot just operate in the home environment for too long, especially since it can become extremely lonely and boring sometimes. You have to really work out what works for you and what does not. The main idea is to create multiple streams of income for yourself, so that you will always have an alternative source of money all the time. Many people in business have realised that once you start a business it creates an opening for other businesses. I have discovered a few avenues to create multiple income streams and I found out that businesses can be seasonal; when you do have multiple income streams there are more avenues available for you to earn income so that you don't become reliant on just one income stream.

Many people are creating multiple streams of income for themselves by building for themselves and their homes a future they desire and the present that they really want. The desire to write this book arose from the need that exists -and a desire to let others know of ways of making money from home. I have met so many people who feel handicapped and who keeps asking me how I manage to stay at home with two kids, the answer is creating multiple streams of income doing what we enjoy doing best.

How do I start my home based business?

Planning for a home based business start up might be a bit daunting, and you might be unsure about where to start from. It is very true that everybody knows something about something, and passion plus skill and talent can generate income for you when you back it up with hard work. There is always a need to be filled and someone definitely needs the skills you have acquired over time to help them solve their problems. When you create a platform for this problem to be solved and you get paid for it then a new business is born.

Brainstorm your skills and talents:

First of all you need to be able to assess your talent. What are you good at? Focus on how you can use both the skills you've acquired over time, and your inherent talents to make your home based business start up a reality. What are those personality traits that drive your passion? Are you creative? Could you make jewelleries to sell or could you create a beautiful gift basket to sell? Are you good with the needle? Do you love writing and you could maybe write an eBook? Are you able to pay great attention to details and do you possess organizational skills and would love bookkeeping, data entry? Maybe the buzz of sales keeps you on your feet and you could try drop-shipping, mail order, and e-marketing? Don't limit yourself to a few options, think of as many options as possible. The truth about business is that one business creates open doors to other businesses. Are you resilient and could you take up telemarketing thereby creating businesses for other people over the phone and making money for yourself.

Don't ever feel that you are not able to do something because you have abilities that are a solution to things that needs your skills. Think of the skills you have acquired over the years and the talents that you have, and then make a list of all the home based business ideas you can come up with. You need to bear in mind that you want to work at home, so after making your list remove anything that can't be done in a residential home. For example you won't be able to be a door to door sales man or a manufacturer at home. Although there is nothing wrong with this idea if you are mobile and flexible. Being mobile would create more open doors and access to more customers. Do not lose heart if you are not, you can find the perfect business to run from home.

Profitability:

How profitable is your enterprise going to be? You need to be very realistic about this, after all the bottom line for success in any business is making profit. If you are thinking of a home based business start up, you need to think of one that will bring in the income that you need. Make sure that people are willing to pay money for your product, and also that the money paid for it in the month will sustain you and create money for you. If an idea on the list does not satisfy this criterion, especially if it's meant to be your main source of income, you might need to cross it off your list. You need to be ruthless with your list and be candid with yourself but don't be afraid of branching out because nothing ventured nothing gained. If you have researched an idea and you are sure it's going to make money, it may not bring in the kind of money you want immediately and you might need a lot of perseverance and persistence initially. You will need to realise that you need to give yourself a period of grace where you learn the ropes of the business and give room for some mistakes. Mistakes are always bound to happen and you can learn from them and make your business better.

Making a business plan:

A business plan is also a very essential part of a successful home based business start up. The main reason for having a business plan is to assess your main business idea. A plan helps you to research the chances of it becoming a successful business. If after your research, your plan shows your idea is not profitable you might need to drop this idea for another one. You need to follow through on your business plan. Make sure juicy ads don't entice you, make your choice based on good research, this will pay off at the end of the day. There is more on this later, with a template and a guideline to give you an idea of what a plan looks like

Home based partnerships and franchises?

They are not all bad ideas. There are good home based franchises out there, but you need to follow through on your research and make sure you are making an informed choice. Do proper research on the parent company, are they in profit? Is it a reputable company?

Don't make the mistakes of signing any contracts before knowing what you are going in for. Some contracts are made to trap you in, so that it will be impossible for you to get out even when you are running at a loss. You might want to get a lawyer to go through the contract for you, a lawyer will be able to identify such clauses and advice you properly. Proper research now will save you a lot of headaches and heartaches in future. There are home based franchises that allow you to work from home and some others involve some element of travel, you need to make sure that the terms of the franchise and feasibility of running it suits your skills and abilities. A lot of initial research will save you a lot of loss in the long run.

Legalities

When considering a home based business start up, you need to choose a form of business and register your business either as a sole proprietorship, partnership or corporation, and you need to register your business name, if your business has a name other than your own. You should also make sure the type of business you have in mind is okay for your residential area. For example if the home-based business involves manufacturing, or trucks or other vehicles arriving at or leaving your property on a regular basis, you should not be operating in a residential area. This type of disturbance will probably not be smiled upon by your neighbours. Make sure that you have the proper type of insurance if your business will involve people and clients coming in and out of your home.

Home office and space:

There is the need to define the work space for your home based business start up. Most especially if you are going to have clients come in and out of your home. Your work area should look professional and your home should look generally neat and attractive to your customers. Differentiate between your living and work space. Try to separate both while devoting your time to each; this will make life much easier for you and your family. Although sometimes for stay home mums this may not be entirely possible as kids run in and out of this space or you may even prefer to work with the kids in an adjacent space so you can keep an eye on them. Whatever suits you on the long run should not hinder the progress of your business.

Drive and determination:

Running your home based business is not always going to be a piece of cake and you will need all the skills necessary to make your business a success? Research shows that successful business men and women share certain traits and attitudes, such as perseverance, the desire and willingness to take the initiative, competitiveness, self-reliance, a strong need to achieve, and self-confidence. You will need a strong sense of determination, drive, discipline, and desire to run a successful home-based business. Many things are going to make you feel like giving up, but these traits will take you a long way. Late Mary Kay Ash started her multi billion dollars business by writing about a business idea after she left her day job, she managed to turn the idea into big business. Mary Kay is a multibillion dollar business today and it has become a force to be reckoned with in the business world with thousands of worldwide representatives testifying to its success. A great idea or plan is just the beginning. Thomas Edison declared that "Genius was one per cent inspiration and ninety-nine per-cent perspiration." This means any good business rides on the back of hard work. Hard work is one thing and determination to succeed is another, determination will help you keep up with all the unexpected events that running a business might throw at you.

Organisation and networking groups

It's a great idea to join a professional group. If you are working alone from home running a one man business especially in the trying times when the business is still growing, you can feel lost and alone. Joining one of the organizations will open up quite a few opportunities for you. Joining one will give you the opportunity of mixing with like minded people, who will give you loads of ideas and information on how to make your business a success. They will offer you support as well in helping you cope with different situations and challenges. This will give you the opportunity to network, build camaraderie and have access to a knowledge bank for solving technical problems. Some franchises give an opportunity or a forum for franchises to meet up or discuss issues that will help them move their business forward.

There are so many opportunities and benefits gained from joining a business organization, benefits range from gaining group support to getting business advice.

This groups give you support since you are starting out on your own business you are able to gain advice from others who might have more experience than you. There are also additional benefits in joining some business organizations such as discounts on particular services or products, or special promotional opportunities. A lot of benefits include giving your business credibility in the eyes of your customers; generally customers view membership with some main organizations as a plus and a sign of credibility. A lot of small business associations also offer the members opportunity to advertise free on their main websites as well as been listed in their business directory for free. You could also have the opportunity of receiving free business advice when you are a part of some of these small business organizations.

There are also online groups. The information highway opens up doors to business-related newsgroups, forums, and mailing lists these online groups can also be a great source of support, networking opportunities, and information exchange. If you are in business already, try joining a group this week, join one of the small business organizations or networking group this week, either off-line or online, especially if you are feeling a little lost. If you are not sure about how to find the right small business associations to join, you can try Yahoo groups, Google directory, and Dmoz online directory. A quick search for home businesses or small businesses will bring up a list of different groups to look at.

HOW TO WRITE A BUSINESS PLAN

As mentioned earlier writing a business plan is essentially in the good interest of any new business. A business plan helps keep things in perspective and gives focus to any business. A business plan should always be current and progressive, and there can always be room for improvement in the plan as the business progresses. A lot of people wonder what the components of a good business plan are, and also how long the business plan should be. Basically the length of a business plan should not really be estimated according to the number of pages, but in the completeness of the whole business plan and in the information it supplies. It should in totality be well summarized and its reader should be able to understand its content. It should be a synopsis of well carried out research that shows the business owner a clear picture of the progress of the business. A good plan varies in length some are shorter than others. The business plan for a large corporate body might run into a hundred pages, while a start up company may be around 20, easy to read, well-spaced text, formatted in bullets, illustrated by business charts and short financial tables plus financial details in appendices.

Some people wonder if they should give it out to a professional to write up for them. Some prefer to write it up themselves and buy business software. First of all depending on the budget this option might be quite expensive, so if you are on a low capital and budget you might want to rule out this option. If you want to use business software, then you should look for the software that will help fulfil the aim of what your business plan was initially intended for. You can easily search for such software's on the internet.

Components of a business plan

There is no fixed content for a business plan. The components of a business plan depend basically on what the business plan is basically intended for and also on its audience. According to the small business association, a good business plan should include something about each of the following.

- o Executive Summary
- o Vision
- o Objectives
- o Present status
- o Market Analysis
- o Company Description
- o Marketing & Sales Management
- o Service or Product Line
- o Financials
- o Appendix

You can check the small business association (SBA) website for more information in business plans. For further research the SBA gives good information in the form of sample business plans and tutorials. It is a great website with great resource. There is a sample business plan and template in appendix 2 this is just a basic sample and guideline. You should do more research into getting a plan that will suit you and your business.

HOME BUSINESS IDEAS

Having dealt with the plans necessary to start up the business, I have researched a list of marketable home business ideas. These ideas have been researched, and are quite marketable depending on your skills and experience. Any type of business will require further research and hard work. If you find that you are interested in any of these businesses, you will need to carry our further research of your own to make sure that this business is viable enough for you.

1. Medical transcription /legal transcription

The medical transcriptionist or legal transcribers are people responsible for converting medical or legal records into typewritten format rather than handwritten. There is more information on this later on in this manual. There's generally no formal education required, but training can be gained through different certification courses, and distance certification courses. This business can easily be set up in your home if you have the required skills and background.

2. Home based business franchises

Running a home based franchise can really be easier than imagined. It allows you use somebody else's already tried and tested business model to run your business. Usually for a royalty fee and a percentage of the gross monthly sales, you'll have the right to sell the franchisors product, and trademark as well. There are so many types of franchises available, so you can choose the right franchise to suit your needs. We have more information and resource on what you need to know about how to set up your franchise.

3. Home based internet opportunities

You can start earning money online. Running a home based internet business is one of the more common home based businesses being run these days. It's a relatively good way to earn a steady stream of income if you know how. There are various avenues available to earning money using the internet. Many examples range from joining quality affiliate programs, blogging, taking paid surveys, running an eBay store, having an online auction site or generally running a websites with ad sense or pay per click (PPC) more on these ideas below.

4. Home based data entry

You can break through the wall of data entry business. A lot of people think it's a daunting task to get into the world of running a well established data entry business from home. A few tips are important though, mainly because there is a lot of competition out there with lots of people who have basic data entry skills. Data entry work involves typing information from something in a hard copy format. The main secret is to improve and add to your basic skills. You can do this by gaining easy to learn specialised skills to help you establish your home based data entry business. Skills such as knowing how to use major database software, like the MS Access and FileMaker Pro, or other skills such as HTML knowledge, Programming experience, Proofreading and so on will make a whole lot of difference, typing skills is also necessary as well. There are so many easy ways to acquire this type of skills, and for the rewards you get it's worth the effort.

Many companies will sub-contract their data entry projects. There is such a dependence on computers these days that it opens up a large avenue for this sort of opportunity. Data entry opportunities include data entry of accounting information, data entry of warranty and other customer information, data entry of medical or legal information, data entry to create mailing lists. For this sort of business you would need a computer and internet connection and method of communication with the companies that you work for. You can find work by searching on-line for opportunities, although you need to be very wary of internet scams as many juicy ads offering great data entry opportunity on line are scams and you need to stay away from these. To find home based data entry work you can contact companies in your area, companies that produce secretarial services, mailing list companies and printing companies are good companies to contact for this sort of services.

Data entry business at home has stressful aspect such as tough deadlines to meet as well as strict accuracy measures to follow. Don't be too hard on yourself if you lack in some skills as you can always take courses to brush up such skills and you can always hire out work that requires a matter of urgency if you can't meet up.

5. Home based gift basket business

Home based gifts business offers so many opportunities for making income. People are always on the lookout for that perfect gift. It's easy to customize a gift basket and, it continues to be an appealing option for many occasions such as birthdays, weddings, baby births, anniversaries, house warming and, romantic occasions. It's a good means of saying thank you and also to celebrate a mile stone in one's life. It needs a relatively low start up capital, you basically need to know what kind of gifts are relevant for what occasions and you could do a lot of marketing through referrals from friends and relatives. Other ways are gift packs at parties for children, many parents don't have a knack for this and don't know what sort of gifts to include in the gift packs for their children's parties, they would gladly contract this out to someone who knows how to produce lovely party packs.

6. Work from home telemarketing business

Telemarketing jobs done from home are called virtual telemarketing jobs and there are many companies that hire virtual help through the Internet. Someone who wants a virtual telemarketing position needs a computer, land-line phone and Internet access. Having a telephone headset is also a good idea. It is however necessary to watch out for good companies with quality products. Some companies will offer poor products or are involved in outright scam. It's necessary to do a thorough home work in searching for the real opportunities. The real companies offer great products or good services. It's necessary to have cold calling experience and if you don't then it's necessary to love making phone calls because this business entails making lots of cold calls. You will also be able to handle negative responses because it is common to get negative responses when making cold calls. The great thing about this type of business is that it's in great demand because these calls generate business and clients that produce the sales of products and services. Many businesses will not even exist without telemarketers. Telemarketers produce clients who are the life wire of any business. To succeed as a telemarketer you need to be confident and professional and you need to have excellent phone manners.

7. Home based travel business

This is a real avenue to make money and be your own boss. Since it involves you booking holidays, it's very necessary for you to be affiliated with travel agencies. You might choose one good agency or decide to have a relationship with a few. You will be an independent contractor, working for yourself and make money on commissions. There is more information on this type of business later.

8. Home based catering business

If you have experience in the catering industry, this will be a plus for your home based catering business. If not you can have someone in the know how to show you the ropes. It's necessary to find out about the legalities of this business in your state and where you live. You might need to make sure it's okay for you to cook from your own kitchen. You will find that catering can provide a good stream of income. You can cater for cocktails, wedding parties, birthday parties, large parties, small parties, depending on what type of experience you have. You can get your initial customers through catering for friends and family and through referrals.

9. Home based jewellery business

Like any home based business, it takes dedication to start a home based jewellery business. It gives you the opportunity to show your creative side by creating lovely pieces of jewellery, and have the satisfaction of seeing people paying money for your lovely creation. Jewellery business could involve doing shows to display and sell your work, it's therefore necessary to learn the art of jewellery display that will bring allure to your work. You'll also want to know how to take professional photographs of your work for your website, auction listings or literatures such as jewellery catalogues. There are kits available to teach and train you on how to create lovely jewellery pieces. You will need to have an eye for detail and a passion for creating art. There are many people who create necklaces earrings, bracelets from precious stones or pearls. They are also able to sell these pieces on their websites or on eBay. If you don't have the ability to create jewelleries but love to sell them, you can search for people with this sort of creative abilities, they might be ready to create the jewelleries while you market and sell them and you split the profit in between yourselves.

10. Home based mail order business/drop shipping

Mail order simply means the buying of goods or services by mail delivery. The buyer places an order with the merchant through the internet, and products are shipped directly to address supplied by customer. Rather than having a lot of inventory, you can make things much easier by selling merchandise through a drop-ship arrangement. This third party such as a manufacturer or wholesaler sells you the merchandise but keeps it in his warehouse and delivers it to your customer for you after you've made the sale. This business is quite lucrative if accompanied with hard work and research of the niche of interest. There are many advantages to drop shipping. Firstly you are able to create your own business with very little risk attached. You don't need to invest much money by letting a shop or buying capital, if any product is not selling well then you don't have a lot of stock holding up your money. You don't have to worry about logistics like shipping and packaging; all these are taken care of by someone else. You can set your own pricing structure to suit your margins. You do need to do a lot of research to locate good products, since you don't have an inventory of stock; you need to make sure the products you are subscribing to are of excellent quality. You will earn yourself a bad name if poor products are shipped out to your customers. Since you will be working from home you need a website that ranks well on the internet and that has good traffic or you could also run this with a catalogue that you send out to customers. You can spread word about your business through word of mouth, referrals and through family and friends. Online auction sites like eBay provide drop ship services as well and you might want to go through this route.

You need to be sure that back ordering does not occur so that you don't lose customers out of frustration. Back ordering is when a seller places a shipment request with a wholesaler, but the product is sold out. This leaves customers frustrated and you will lose customers this way. It is your responsibility to be aware of the quantity of products available with the wholesaler. You need to monitor this so that your products are always available. You also need to monitor shipping times to make sure that your customers get their products on time.

You need to be aware of scams, make sure you research for legitimate wholesalers, you might want to inspect the wholesalers business by inspecting the site and location to ascertain its viability and to make sure it is legitimate. Some scammers will provide a list of wholesalers, this people will end up not been wholesalers but middlemen who have no product to sell, this will inflate the price of item, elongate the process and these scammers may even send substandard items to your customers, so doing your research well is key to the success of this type of business .

11. Home based sewing business

Home based sewing business. Are you inventive, creative with sewing skills? This might just be the home based business for you. You can carry out embroidery work, alterations, sewing and charge money for this. You can also incorporate sewing into an existing cloths business. If for example you sell wedding gowns, suits or brides maid dresses you can incorporate alterations and fitting into the business, people always need to be fitted prior to weddings and this will boost sales in this sort of business. You can also sew suits and have them ordered on your websites. Custom made suits are definitely in vogue, and people pay a handsome fee for this sort of suits. Some people have websites set up so that customers can access this easily. Customers are able to input all necessary information in-to these sites, data necessary for the suits production such as: their sizes, type of material and the design of suit they are interested in are all inputted into the site. They place their order on these sites, however this might be a bit tricky as alterations might be necessary on the suits, but this can be easily sorted. You can even offer incentives like free shipping if necessary to sort out the alterations. To run a custom-made suit website successfully you need to have a suitable website that allows your customers access you and makes it easy for your customers to input the necessary information. You also need to be a good tailor or know someone who will sew suits beautifully and for a fee.

12. Customer service business from home

A lot of big companies hire virtual customer service agents who work from home running their own business according to the company's guidelines. These companies constantly hire customer service agents. This form of outsourcing has opened up opportunities for those who want to work from the comfort of their own home. You will need to be a self starter with exceptional customer service skills. Many companies who offer this sort of outsourcing opportunities even offer training if you lack the skills required. You are responsible for providing and maintaining your own computer, land line and high-speed Internet service, just as you would be for any home-based business. Those costs are not covered or reimbursed. When you successfully get a virtual interview with a company offering this sort of opportunity, treat it like any normal interview, be professional. No background noise like crying babies, barking dogs, or TV noises.

There are various opportunities for people in search of jobs of customer service nature from home, I have listed a few companies listed below, and they offer to hire those with customer service skills and who will like to work from home. These customer service jobs might be just what you are looking for. It's very important that you meet the requirements and possess the necessary qualifications before applying for these positions. These opportunities allow you to build your business around your home life; some of the opportunities allow you to choose the times you want to work as well. The equipments you need most times are a good working computer, head sets and microphone and internet connection. Some of the companies that offer you this opportunity will train you, some training might be free and some might be for a fee. You will more than likely need a quiet area to work effectively, free of noise and distractions from your TV or your children. Some companies that offer this sort of opportunities are below.

Alpine access - Customer service representatives

Arise - Customer service representatives

Live Ops - Customer service representatives

13. Home based Pet business

Year after year, the pet supply industry exceeds expectations and grows by nearly 2 Billion dollars. Anyone even can take advantage of this growing market and own an online pet store. You might want to go down the franchise route. Some franchises opportunities are available for this type of business, a franchise might be a good way to start out especially if they offer you great support, but do make sure you go for great products and always carefully check out the legalities of any contract before you sign on to any franchise.

You can sell pet accessories to pet lovers who will definitely come back to your online store for more quality products, we all know how destructive pets can be. There are so many high demand pet products out there for you to choose from: pet treats, grooming products, pet toys, pet health and the list goes on.

Some people have been able to build viable pet businesses that produce for them a steady source of income. Pet grooming is another pet business that you can run in the home. You can run this independent of your pet supply business or alongside it. There is more information later on running a successful home based pet business.

14. Make money as a freelance writer

Freelance writing is another of making money from the comfort of your own home. Many people and corporations will give you money to write articles for them. Many blog owners will pay you money to update their blogs. People will pay you to update their website. Some people are interested in writing eBooks and don't know how, they pay other people to write eBooks for them. If you have the experience you can write editorial for publishers and writing for magazines. This is a business that has a lot of possibilities for those with the experience. If you do not have the experience you can improve your writing and editing skills by taking a course. With a bit of research on your part you will find lots of opportunities depending on your niche and experience. There are many opportunities online for this kind of business as well. There are websites that constantly advertise writing opportunities and with a bit of internet search you will find a lot of these opportunities available to you either through home learning distant routes or other routes that you may choose.

16. Running a child minding business in your home

For those who love children this is a great opportunity to launch a business taking care of kids from your home, offering quality childcare to those that need it, because more parents must work outside the home, there is always a demand for quality child care. You will need to have the necessary training and your home must have the proper government safety standards. You might run this alone or hire someone to work with you in your home. In some places you can also work as a support worker giving new childminders advice and support and getting paid for it. To qualify as a child minder you will be required to register and be approved by the necessary regulatory body. Like any other business this will require your drive, enthusiasm and determination to succeed. You need to check the laws and regulations in your area, there will be a guide to how many children you can take care of and you may be able to hire another qualified person in your home as well. You can advertise your business by word of mouth and referral or by advertising in a local newspaper or online. You may be worried about providing necessary equipments and toys for the children. You can always cut budget by buying pre owned items that are still in very good condition, these items include furnishings, toys, books, games, videos, DVD movies, children's music tapes and CD's from resale shops, garage sales, thrift stores, classified ads, and even on eBay, you will be surprised to see how much money you will save through this.

17 Making money as a virtual assistant

You can render help as a virtual assistant to small offices that do not have secretaries or PA's. There is a lot you can offer with your computer, phone line and internet connection. You will be providing excellent administrative or technical support remotely to people and businesses that require this type of help. You will need to have a good marketing strategy this will help your business to grow. Initially you might need to work long hours as well as non-traditional times. The great thing is that with technology at your finger tips you can operate globally having clients across the country and beyond. A virtual assistant saves employers money, time, training, working space, taxes and so on. Once you have made up your mind to go down this route, decide what sort of service you are ready to offer, develop a niche or area that you can master so that you will be on top of the game in this area. Carry out a thorough research to find out who needs this kind of service in your area. Conduct a market survey so that you will be sure of its marketability and profitability. Market your service continuously so you can be an established brand. Join an organisation or group to help you with marketing and development.

This type of remote assistance can be in different forms and there are different software's that enables you to operate remotely. You will be able to access your clients' computers, calendars, emails and contacts as well. Many virtual assistants also provide web development, design and maintenance, desktop publishing, meeting and event planning, bookkeeping, and business start-up consultations. You can book meetings, and make travel plans. The services are endless depending upon your knowledge, skills and capabilities, skills like typing, web design, graphic arts and writing. You can offer technical help desk support from your home with the adequate type of technology, you will be resolving technical issues for this customers. A lot of skills can be useful to a virtual assistant and there are many ways these skills can be used to help your customers.

HOME BASED MEDICAL TRANSCRIPTION

Home medical transcription provides a lot of opportunities out there for lovers of data entry as well as legal transcription jobs opportunities. Preparation is needed for success in this area; you will need to have training to effectively carry out this business. There is also the need to have the necessary equipments to set up this business in your home. As mentioned previously, formal education is not required but there are different routes for certification and training.

Home based medical transcription equipments?

To set up you need to have some required basic pieces of equipment.

The Basic equipments needed to start a home medical transcription business are:

1. **Hardware required for home medical transcription**

    a. Computer
        i.   RAM – Minimum 256 MB
       ii.   Hard Disk – Minimum 20 GB

      iii.   CPU – Minimum 2.2 GHz
  b. Foot Pedal
  c. Ear phones
  d. Amplifier

I will definitely recommend a high memory storage capacity for your system from about 512 MB of RAM or above, this is mainly because while transcribing a medical report you would need to open multiple applications like medical dictionary, spell checker, word, IE, est. simultaneously. So you can see that a higher memory will allow good speed, smoother work and fewer headaches, while a lower memory capacity will slow down your work.

2. **Software's required for Home Medical Transcription**

  a. Preferable WinXP,
  b. Microsoft Office 2000
  c. Medical Dictionaries
  d. Spell Checker
  e. Line Counter application for invoicing

MEDICAL TRANSCRIPTIONISTS INCOME

There is a real earning potential with medical transcription jobs at home, although how much you really earn depends on a whole lot of factors, depending on how much work you take on and how flexible you are. A skilled medical transcriptionist who works at his or her own home usually makes more income than one who works in a traditional job setting or at an online service. This is because home based workers can have their own accounts and take on a lot of work; they may also choose to limit the amount of work they decide to take on to suit their schedule.

The amount a medical transcriptionist earns also depends on his or her years of experience. If you run your own business you will be able to control your earnings more, there will be fluctuations in your earnings though depending on how much contracts you are able to take on. If you do run your own business the early period may not be very lucrative, mainly because you will still be trying to expand your business and will most likely still be learning the ropes of running your own business while trying to gain more contracts. With time as your business grows you will be able to hire subcontractors and take on more work and hence make more money.

Independent contractors earn more than transcriptionists who work for employers, but independent contractors have higher expenses than office workers. Methods of payment differs as well, some transcriptionists are paid wages and the wages paid depends on the number of lines transcribed or the number of hours spent working, this method of payment is much better for an experienced worker who will be able to take on more work. Another mode of payment is a standard per-hour basic pay, this standard payment might be better for a new starter just starting out, this will give the new starter guaranteed income. The most common method of payment is pay "per line" of transcription. This depends on the length of experience level of the Medical Transcriptionists (MT) the type of job, and the turn-around time required by the physician which is usually between 24 to 48hrs.

MEDICAL TRANSCRIPTION TRAINING

The rising popularity of the medical transcription jobs brings up a lot of questions about the type of training required to be a success in this field. Like most job hunting experience, there is always an amount of effort required to get your feet off the ground. A lot of the transcription companies look to hire people with the training and experience. It's quite essential to have good experience and training background to be ahead in the game. Most times good experience is gained in the medical field such as hospitals and clinics. The on-the-job experience will be gained in a medical environment such as in a hospital or clinic. There is the need to understand the medical language been used during dictation? There can be no compromise made with accuracy due to the impact it would have on patient records. Proof of training and education can be shown by doing a certification course and passing the exams. During your training, your transcription courses will focus on medical language, including the Greek and Latin roots of medical terms. You'll be expected to develop a working knowledge of medical practices as well.

During your medical transcription training the courses should allow you gain a very good understanding of medical documents such as patient histories, examination records, consultations, and discharge papers. It's also very important for you to understand the medical laws for you to be able to produce official medical records. Obviously you'll need to develop your computer skills as well. To understand and accurately transcribe dictated reports your training should be expected to train you in courses such as anatomy and physiology, diagnostic procedures, pharmacology, and treatment assessments. If you are based within the US and Canada, during the medical transcription training the medical transcription courses you will take, should prepare you to take the Certified Medical Transcriptionist exam.

It's essential to look out for genuine programs that will offer you the quality educational training that you require. There are good opportunities out there, if you are on the lookout for good training make sure your emphasis lies on quality, find out programs that will offer you quality training to include all of the above and more.

HOME BASED BUSINESS FRANCHISE

There are different types of home based franchises available, giving you a wide variety to choose from, if you want to go down the franchise route. There is a long list of popular franchises, and what you might need to do when considering a franchise.

Choosing a franchise

Making the right choice involves doing a balanced and thorough research. It's initially basically the same as researching into starting up any business. The main difference in actuality is the franchise agreements and different contracts that make the franchise business unique. You need to think about the resources you have available, most franchise require a level of investment and you need to be sure that you have enough for this, if not you might think about the option of taking out an affordable loan. Once you have been able to conclude on how much investment you can put into your business, this will help you narrow down your options based on the franchise investment you can afford.

Once you've narrowed down your options to the field and industry that interests you. Check out the top home based franchises for this field in the geographic area where you live, visit franchise trade shows, ask questions stopping at various booths at the trade show to get more information. Once you have a list of home based franchises that interest you, request for information from these companies to have a proper feel for what the franchise is all about. You can find out if it's possible to set up a first interview with one of the consultant to talk you through what they do, and how they operate the business. At this prelimnary stage you can ask as many questions as possible, don't limit yourself to a few questions and don't be afraid to ask as many questions as possible, remember it's still early days and you are still investigating and researching your options.

It's very important that you do your own investigation about the home based franchises you are thinking of, do not make the mistake of relying just on the information they give you, remember you need to protect your interest as well as your investment. Do a bit of detective fact finding on the company you are thinking of. Find out from consumer or franchise regulators in your area to see if there are any serious problems with the company you're considering. Is it a profitable enterprise? Find out if they are a reputable company, find out if they have delivered good services in the past. At the initial interview ask if it's possible to talk to few franchisees, ask for a list of franchisees so you can randomly pick from the list, this will help you get non-based information about the company. Pre-plan your questions and write down a list of all the questions you have for the franchisor. Question the franchisor about the territory; find out if the territory will be for your sole and exclusive use. Find out what form of training and assistance you will get from the company. You might want to find out how they stay ahead of competitors, and what threats the company might be facing for the services offered in the market place. Find out how grievances with franchisees are handled by the company. Ask about ongoing fees and how they are charged; also find out how much you will need to contribute to advertising campaigns if at all you have to. You should also want to know if any of the company's franchisees have failed in the past and what contributed to the failure. Carry out extensive research and compare different franchises to find out the ones that have good packages, the more you get for your money the better.

Agreements and contracts:

Once you've had interviews with the franchisor and also with existing franchisees, examination of the audited financial statements is very important. An earnings-claim statement, profit-and-loss statement is another important document that you need to examine, all these are quite necessary to determine the financial status of the company in question and to determine if past franchisees are in profit or not. You should not be afraid of asking for these documents from the franchisor, it's important for you to protect your interest. There is no particular format for contract or legal document in the United Kingdom but if based in the United States a copy of Franchise Disclosure Document-FDD is an important document that you need to ask for. It's essential for the franchisee to look through all these early enough during the transaction and not dump this essential document in a corner. If possible you might want to get a professional to look through it for you. All franchisors must provide the FDD to potential franchisees at least 10 days before the signing of any agreement – This legal document contains the details and documents listed below.

- The Franchisor and Any Predecessors
- Litigation History
- Bankruptcy (i.e. any franchisees who may have filed)
- Listing of the Initial Franchise Fee and Other Initial Payments
- Other Fees and Expenses
- Statement of Franchisee's Initial Investment
- Obligations of Franchisee to Purchase or Lease from Designated Sources
- Obligations of Franchisee to Purchase or Lease in Accordance with Specifications or from Authorized Suppliers
- Financing Arrangements
- Obligations of the Franchisor, Other Supervision, Assistance or Services
- Exclusive/Designated Area of Territory
- Trademarks, Service Marks, Trade Names, Logotypes and Commercial Symbols
- Patents and Copyrights
- Obligations of the Franchisee to Participate in the Actual Operation of the Franchise Business

- Restrictions on Goods and Services Offered by Franchisee
- Renewal, Termination, Repurchase, Modification and Assignment of the Franchise Agreement and Related Information
- Arrangements with Public Figures
- Actual, Average, Projected or Forecasted Franchise Sales, Profits or Earnings
- Information Regarding Franchises of the Franchisor
- Financial Statements
- Contracts
- Acknowledgment of Receipt by Respective Franchisee

You need to thoroughly examine the franchise agreement of any of the home based franchises you've chosen. You will probably need to contact an attorney whose experienced eye will highlight and point out to you important parts of the agreement that you need to be aware of. An attorney will show and explain the meaning of all the legal terms of the contract. An attorney will also show what activities will violate the term of the contract. The terms of the contract will tell you what training you will get from them, what sort of advertisement is acceptable and how much you may have to put towards local and national advertisement campaigns. It usually contains the operating manual that tells you everything about how the business is to be run. It will tell you how the book keeping is to be done. It should establish that you'll be paying an ongoing percentage of sales, or a fixed monthly or annual amount to the franchisor for been a part of the company. It should also establish how long the contract will be for and terms of renewal or termination of the contract on the part of the franchisors. Some franchisors also put a clause that disallows you from opening an identical business to safeguard their secrets from been divulged during the contract or for a period of time after contract has expired, this might be dangerous territories because you will not be able to carry out any similar business. The necessity of researching the business and its contracts cannot be over emphasized, contracts are binding and once signed you may be in serious trouble if you violate the terms.

EARN MONEY ONLINE

You can earn money online, whether you are a student or a stay at home mum, retired or disabled without having much mobility. The earning possibilities the web offers are endless. Many people are making money on the internet right from the comfort of their own homes so why can't you? Make money from your website, join affiliate programs, get paid to take online surveys, get paid by reading emails, earn revenue by placing ads on your Website, advertisement programs, get a fee to refer customers, receive commission for offering custom builds, run a blog, sell your web templates and logos, power sell on eBay and so on.

Paid surveys: You can earn money taking online surveys. I know you have probably wondered if it's really possible to earn money online by taking surveys. Well people are making money every day by taking paid surveys. You can actually join paid membership sites that allow you to be a member of their survey club for a small amount. You are able to take as many surveys as you like for a good sum. You just need to be careful about the different scam offers out there. There is more information on these.

Blogging: You can also start to earn money online by starting up a blog, make your blog an avenue for people to add their various inputs through their comments. Try an interesting idea that will get people stopping by your blog or even bookmarking it for regular visits. Companies will pay you money to advertise their products and services on your blog.

Write an eBook: Don't worry! It's not as difficult as you think. You can write an eBook about almost anything, write about something that you know and love and earn money online. It's very possible to sell a few thousand copies of your eBook; you can even pay a good marketer to do it for you. People will pay online for the eBook and download it. You don't have to worry about publishing and printing. You can sell your eBook through affiliate programs in places like click bank. Affiliates will sell the book for you on commission basis. Amazon will publish and market your book for you although you might need to pay royalty fees.

Affiliate programs: Affiliate marketing basically is an Internet-based marketing practice through which a business rewards one or more affiliates for each visitor or customer brought about by the affiliate's marketing efforts. A good example is Google ad sense. This displays ads supplied by Google on private websites, and then pays those website owners for the privilege. You can also become an eBay affiliate by joining the eBay affiliate program. You partner with eBay to show item listings or eBay links on your website that are relevant to its content, and eBay will pay you a commission for new memberships and for sales that occur when users clicked through from your website, you don't have to sell anything on eBay to make money as their affiliate.

Website design: You can use your graphic skills in designing websites to earn money online. You can create designs, web templates; use your HTML, CSS skills. With good marketing skills, you can sell this to webmasters who are interested in trying out new web template designs but don't have the time or skills required to do the designing themselves. With your graphic skills you can create logos and icons which can be sold online.

Write a newsletter: If you have the patience for a project that will need patience and perseverance, you can try making money on the internet by writing a quality newsletter on your website. It's essential that your newsletter is of excellent quality this will attract a very long list of free subscribers. The more quality content you provide the more subscribers you have. With a long list of subscribers you will get advertisers who will pay you a good sum of money to be featured in you newsletter. This is more of a project that will take time to grow because you need a large list of subscribers before you get any serious advertisers but if you are determined this will pay off on the long run. Once you have a large list of subscribers you will find it relatively easy to solicit for adverts on your websites.

Freelance Work: Earn money on line and take on work such as freelance writing. If you possess a high level of written English then it's easy to get started and all you need are the necessary qualities and any word processing software such as Open Office, Abiword or

Microsoft Word. As mentioned earlier you can also earn money online and freelance as a virtual assistant. You will be a great help to many small businesses who need help running their business but don't have enough hands on deck. You will do things like making reservations, paying bills, booking appointments and meetings all from your home. You can also freelance as an eBay trading assistant and make money off commissions.

Power sell through eBay: Earn money online by becoming an ebayer, (more on this below), the possibilities are endless on eBay. Sell your old goods rather than throw them away, clear your attic and sell those things you've kept away for years. For example sell your old baby stuff on eBay if the baby making years are over. If you don't have the time, you can join the trading assistant program and enlist the help of an eBay trading assistant, you can read more information on how to make money on eBay later on in this manual.

EARN MONEY TAKING SURVEYS

WHY WILL THE COMPANIES PAY ME?

You can earn money taking online surveys. How? A lot of companies need product certainty before launching their products this is called survey research. It doesn't matter how well established a company is, they still need to make sure that their products will sell in the open market. For a product to be really successfully it has to fill a need or else people won't buy the products. Companies not only need your opinion, but their success relies on your opinion, so a lot of big companies are prepared to invest money in good surveys for this purpose.

IS IT FOR YOU?

The true fact is that not everyone is able to take part in online surveys. Some people are not able to sit down for so long at a stretch. You need to ask yourself if you are able to take part in surveys without pulling your hair out at the end of the day.

HOW TO GET SET UP

To get set up for taking surveys, it's advisable to open an email solely for the purpose of the surveys, this helps to get you organized. You need to be aware that there are scams out there so you need to carefully make your choice. After doing your research properly and you have made up your mind about the good survey opportunities, then sign up with as many survey companies as possible. If you fill out just a few you will only get limited offers. They will ask you to fill a survey questionnaire to help them know what sort of surveys to send to you. It is very important to fill in the correct information and give enough information because if you don't it will limit the amount of surveys sent to you, and also the amount of money you make. Once you are all set up then you can start to earn money taking online surveys.

FREE SURVEYS OR PAID SURVEY WEBSITES?

If you are really serious and will like to earn money taking online surveys, you should think about joining the paid survey websites. You will not earn enough from the free surveys, you will only make some cash and probably win a few prizes. The reason why paid survey companies are now well sought after is because they only take on legitimate companies for inclusion into their database and send out decent surveys, so you don't waste your time and effort looking for the good surveys to take part in. You can make much more by joining focus groups and online discussions, also online fill-in surveys, phone surveys, video conference call surveys. These opportunities are only available through paid survey sites. A focus group is a group of people who are brought together to discuss a particular item for an hour or so and they do get paid a fair sum for taking part in this focus groups. If you are more interested in the free surveys then a Google search will bring you different free surveys to choose from. If you go down the paid survey route, be careful not to join scam sites, be very wary of sites advertised by pop up adverts, they are usually not legitimate. They may just be sites that solicit for personal information of who ever accesses them, they sell this information to third party marketing sites who will end up bombarding you with spam. If you choose the paid routes make sure that you read the fine prints so that you know what exactly you are going for.

MAKE MONEY BLOGGING

It's not a far-fetched idea making money blogging. Blogging is a good way to make money on the internet, it's not however a get rich quick scheme, it takes dedication, hard work, patience and passion. You should also have a clear business model for your blog. You will need an audience that will fall in love with your blog. It's much better to solve real problems on your blog, and have a good understanding of who your audience are and what their needs are. If you provide relevant content that continually solves real issues, then you will have traffic of people and you will be able to monetize easily. The more audience you have the more successful your blog is going to be and the easier it will be to monetize it.

A lot of people don't know the first thing about blogging, or ways of making money blogging. They probably don't know how to start or what to write about. The first thing is finding a topic that is of great interest to you, this will make the whole experience a more pleasurable one because you will be writing on what you love and with a good business model get paid for it. It could be anything that range from photography, pets food, health, you name it. Once you find a topic then find out what the real issues are in these areas you would then want to build relevant content that address these issues in your blog. You need to be at the cutting edge of your chosen topic releasing the latest news; buzz on whatever it is that your niche is all about.

Setting up

1. You need to consider good web hosting, not just a cheap host that will set you up with a bad quality blog, but one that will give you a whole desirable package to run and maintain the website and keep you in business, examples are MuseCrafters.com, Livejournal.com, JournalHome.com, Blogger, Choselt, WordPress.com, TheDiary.org, Mindsay.com, Blog.ir, Blogagotchi.com, Diaryland.com, Blogdrive.com, weebly.com or Xanga.com. Most are easy to set up without the need of much technical know how.

2. Once you've set up with a good host you need to choose your niche, as explained above choose something you love, something that you will always be able to give current information about. You should also work with a niche that's broad enough for a good audience but not too broad for you to handle, this makes it easy to capture the niche and ultimately an easier way of making money blogging. Google has a keyword tool that you can use for your niche search and your key word search. For your blog you would want to use good keywords that will make relevant audience find your blog out of the millions others out there.

Monetising your blog

Once you have set up your blog and you now have a general idea of how to get all set up on how to write up a good blog, you should be thinking of how to make money with your blog. You need to have a good business model, and think of multiple streams of income. There are many ways you can make money through your blog.

1. You can utilize the pay-per click advertising route such as the Google ad sense, on your blog to generate income; there are also different advertising programs that you can run on your site such as kontera, bidvertiser, auctionads and so on.

2. You can choose the affiliate route way of making money blogging. You have a product related site you can direct your traffic through affiliate programs to make money on your blog examples click bank, Amazon affiliate program among others. There is more information on this in the affiliate marketing section.

3. Another good way of making money blogging is utilizing private ad sales/ sponsorships, with this kind of program different private entities pay to place adverts and run different campaigns on parts of your blog site.

4. Another good way of making money blogging is the "get paid to blog route", once you've maintained your blog for a while and you have a Google Page Rank, link profile and Alexa Rank then you can Submit all of your blogs to multiple get paid to blog websites like Blogitive, Blogsvertise, Review Me, Sponsored Reviews,

PayperPost, LoudLaunch. Then start writing sponsored posts where you can.

5. You might also decide that rather than setting up your own blog site you want to join a blog network, here you will be paid to maintain, create contents for blogs.

6. You can get a job as a blogger and get paid for it, a lot of businesses and companies are hiring specialist bloggers for their websites and this bloggers are getting paid for these services.

Blogging carnivals, what are they?

You should find out about blogging carnivals, these are very effective ways of getting popularity within your niche as well as traffic. Periodically submit your best blog posts to the appropriate carnivals for your niche. Carnivals are easy ways to get links and traffic, and best of all, they're free, and could sky rocket your traffic, if you are just starting out, you can submit your blog once per week.

Don't limit yourself

Finally you don't have to limit your site to just a blog, you can also start making money blogging by building a whole website and targeting your blogs with the content of your website. This will bring a whole new type of traffic to your site, people who are not really into blogs but will be more willing to take a look at a website for information. For this purpose you need to carefully choose a host that will meet your needs and

also you need to create great content for this site as
well.

MAKE MONEY THROUGH AFFILIATE MARKETING

Affiliate marketing definition?

There is so much buzz about affiliate marketing these days, and one might wonder what the buzz is all about. Basically it's the means of market penetration through websites. These websites target specific groups of internet users. It's another means of making money through the internet. To get into the affiliate marketing business, you will need a strong online presence through a website; you will also need to have a business relationship with a business merchant who will allow you to have a link on your website. When your visitors click on the link and subsequently make a purchase from the merchant, you receive a commission based on the amount of the sale, a referral fee or a pay-per-click fee depending on the type of affiliate program. There is more information on pay-per click.

Reputable affiliate programs

The affiliate marketing definition goes further to include the definition of who an affiliate is and also of who the affiliate merchant is. An affiliate is the owner of the website, basically if you own the website with the merchants link in it then you become an affiliate and the merchant whose link is on your website becomes the affiliate merchant. The affiliate markets the goods and products of the merchants through their website. As an affiliate, it's quite important to get linked up to reputable companies with reputable products. You don't want to be linked up to a fraudulent merchant or one that offers bad products to customers; this will definitely spoil business for you. There are many merchants out there that offer reputable affiliate programs. Merchants such as click bank and Amazon offer good affiliate programs.

Going a step further

It's great to understand the affiliate marketing definition, buts it's more important to know how to run a profitable affiliate marketing website. It's quite important to get your customers in the right mood to click on the merchant link on your website, this is called preselling. It's quite important to understand in full the art of affiliate marketing. You need to know how to presell your customers, bearing in mind that you are not actually selling anything you are mainly just redirecting your traffic to the merchants link on your site, so don't get in the hard sell mode with your website rather presell your customers. You need to get your customers presold so that they are ready to click your affiliate link with an open to buy attitude, or in the case of filling out forms then they are primed and ready to click and fill the affiliate forms or click on your ads as the case may be.

What is preselling?

Preselling is prepping the readers and visitors who visit your website by giving them good content to read. This content will lead them to the affiliate links on the websites. For example if you have a website on weight loss, it might make more sense to build a content that gives great advice on weight loss, then adding affiliate links of reputable weight loss programs. If you talk directly about the affiliate products, the visitors might not be interested in clicking your affiliate link because of your hard sell method. Imagine a scenario where you have a weight loss problem, won't you be more interested in buying products from a genuine site that gives you great advice on how to reduce your weight rather than a website that just tells you to buy a particular product because it's a great product? The truth is that you will be more drawn to the sites that take extra time to research and gives you good information.

Content they say is king. One of the best ways to presell your customers and get them in the right mood is to have great content on your website. Great content is attributed to relevance and needed information. Real information that gets the attention of your customers and also a good style of writing that captivates them. There is no point in having an affiliate marketing website with poor content and flashing banners all over the place, it will ultimately drive your traffic and income away, keep your site clean and attractive to readers. Another very important key to the success of your affiliate marketing website is to know your product inside out. Don't take it for granted that since you won't have direct contact with the customers you can take an easy short cut out, the traffic coming to your website can tell easily if you know what you are talking about or not!! It is better not to lose traffic that way.

PAY PER CLICK MARKETING

Pay per click is when you get paid commission when the adverts or affiliate links on your website gets clicked. The most common way of monetising through pay-per click these days is Google ad sense although there are other programs as well, such as the pay per click ads from Yahoo! search marketing. Believe it or not people are making money through the pay per click route. It won't make you an instant millionaire but with time it will yield you income.

One of the good things about the pay per click means is that your site visitor's don't even have to make any purchase, they just have to click on the ads and you start earning commission right away. It's quite important though that you need to develop good content for your website and always remember that "content is king" good content will sustain traffic and the more the traffic to your site, the more the clicks on your ads and ultimately the more the income you get.

If perhaps you've kept a journal over the years on something or if you have some great insight to a relevant topic, it could be any topic really, from fishing to bringing up kids. You can monetise this rather than keeping it away somewhere in your attic. What you need to do is get your domain set up, get in your content, select the best pay-per click option and start getting paid. Your new affiliate website may not get large traffic at the on start but with proper research and keywords placements, you will gradually build traffic to your site, don't get caught up in pay per click affiliate scams promising you brilliant revenues and percentages instantly.

The best way to raise your income as a pay per click affiliate is to set up your websites properly by researching for the right keywords to use. Google ad keywords tool gives you a very good way to research your keywords, especially when combined with some niche finding software's like the micro niche finder and Google keyword tool, you will get good keywords that will draw in the traffic to your site and monetise well. The best keywords that pay per click affiliates use are those that are well targeted. It's quite essential that your sites keywords are well integrated into the contents displayed on the pages of your website, this way you will get a good click through rate because visitors drawn to your content will be naturally drawn to the ads on your site since they will be relevant to what they are searching for.

RUNNING A PET BUSINESS

Pet store and drop shipping/ Pet Grooming business:

If you've been looking for a home based pet business opportunity, why not try an online pet business or a pet grooming business as mentioned earlier. There are different ways to run an online pet store. You can choose to go down the drop shipping route; in this case you are linked to a merchant who owns a large warehouse of pet products. As previously discussed all you need basically is a good website with loads of traffic so when your customers place their orders you send it to the merchant who will then send it to your customer for you. You can run a catalogue service as well to boost product sales. The great thing about having a drop shipping business for your online pet store is that you don't need to create space to store up your products, and you don't have to deal directly with customers. To diversify your income you can also go down the affiliate route. There are so many pet companies that run affiliate programs. You can carefully select the best affiliate programs as well as the most profitable one. When you sign up with an affiliate program you get a link to place on your website for the company. Every click that converts into a sale from your website earns you a commission depending on the contract agreement you've signed up with the company. Don't forget to read the agreements before you sign up though, because some companies will not allow you to run their program on your site along with other programs, so you might want to be careful before signing up with different programmes. To run this business successfully you need to keep yourself up to date with current pet products in the market, subscribe to pets magazines, and attend pet shows.

Another viable pet business is the pet grooming business; many people would pay to have you groom their pets. It can include cleaning the ears, trimming and polishing nails, brushing their teeth, and shave or brush the animal's coat. You may decide to have your clients drop and pick up their pets at your home, or you can drop the pets off for a fee. Pets include cats, dogs, and hamsters. Since there is no certification necessary, there are some pet grooming schools that train people in the skills necessary for this sort of business, some also offer pet grooming business management classes, this is a great additional benefit because you get additional training on how to run your business and make a success of it. There will also be some element of paper work and office work required to keep your business organised.

Make sure you check your local authorities for the necessary license and insurance requirement to setting up this kind of business in your area. Keep your customers happy by offering great customer service, this will keep them coming back to you and they will also refer you to their friends. Capital for this type of start up will be low but you will need to bear in mind that the equipments, licence, training and insurance costs all add up to the cost of running your business. Join associations and online groups that offer advice, and help with training and start ups.

HOME BASED TRAVEL AGENCY

So you've been thinking about becoming a home based travel agent and you're wondering if it is possible to break even in this type of business. According to the Travel Industry Association of America, every second in the United States, thousands of dollars is spent by residents and international tourists on travel and tourism. There really is a lot of resource out there for you and there are associations that by joining will give you the support that you need, you need to do a lot of research on your own to kick-start your business. The basic skills needed in becoming a successful home based travel agent are strong self motivation, great communication skills, computer skills, and a passion for travel, strong sense of determination, self discipline and achievable targets.

Types of home-based travel agent

Basically a home based travel agent is anyone who is involved in selling travel products from a home office and there are different types of travel agents, you can choose to be a cruise only agent, home based agents, give educational tours, become an outside sales representative and so on. As a travel agent, you are your own boss, an independent contractor. For example the home based outside sales representative works with an accredited travel agency, whereby he or she will find customers and qualify their needs, this can easily be done over the telephone from your home office. The host agency who serves as the middle man between the homes based agent and the flight company will then print the tickets, and commission is shared between them.

Presentation

Although you work as a home based travel agent and not from within the walls of an agency, you still need to present your product in a professional and an attractive manner. You are after all a sales professional with a viable product so there is the need for you to present your product in such a way that your clients sees the viability and real essence of buying that product.

Qualifications

As a home based travel agent in the UK you would need to join ABTA, the travel association in the UK, you will need to qualify to be a part of this group, please check their website www.abta.com for details on what you will need to qualify. Joining is for a yearly fee but there is a whole lot of resource in the form of training, tools and support that you will get from being a part of either of these associations. You need to make sure that you are able to run your business from your home. Check with the local authorities in your area to see what is required to set this business up in your home. You can take up the ABTAC travel agent certification courses in local colleges. If you find that you do not qualify to join ABTA you can join groups and organisations that will give you the opportunity to run your own travel business from home. A very good example is the freedom travel group in the UK check the website for this group to find out information, www.freedomtravelgroup.co.uk . Another example is Future travel; there is more information on this group at www.futuretravelcareers.co.uk. These groups offer the opportunity to help you become a home based travel agent. The freedom travel group has different type of packages it also has a package that gives opportunities to newbie's in the industry to join the group, this package allows people with little or no experience in the travel industry to run their home based -travel businesses. With other groups like future travel you will need to have some travel experience along with the ABTAC certification course based on your experience and background.

If you are setting up in the United States, you should look to join associations like the outside sales support network (OSSN) in the United States. Since you are starting the business in on your own you would be an outside sale travel agent. This group allows you to become a member for a fee, and it has in depth information on how to run your independent travel business, for in-depth research into establishing this business in your home information is available at www.ossn.com . You will also want to work towards becoming IATAN qualified, and getting you IATA card and number.

KICKSTARTING YOUR TRAVEL BUSINESS

To get your first customers you should contact your friends, practise your sales pitch on them as well as on your family, old colleagues, club members, friendly neighbours and so on, keep practising your sales pitch on them and keep using them as your bouncing board. Generally pre-think your questions, ask questions on hobbies, where they will like to spend their vacations, with your questions, point them towards your products and convince them that they have made the right decisions by picking on the benefits of your package.

RUNNING A HOME BASED RECRUITMENT COMPANY

Becoming a home based head-hunter is not a very difficult dream to achieve, headhunting could be a profitable business and it can be run from your own home. A day in the life of a successful head hunter or recruiter is a very busy one and should be filled with organised activities. The work space of a head-hunter is a hub of activities especially phone calls both incoming and outgoing. If you want to become a successful head-hunter you have to be very bold and confident over the phone. You will be making a lot of cold calls and outbound calls initially to secure vacancies from employers, so you should be confident enough to talk to key decision makers over the phone. The life wire of headhunting is having vacancies to fill, so there is the continuous need to acquire new businesses over the phone by continuously calling companies for business opportunities. HR outsourcing companies are also good companies to call. HR outsourcing companies are mostly contracted to service the recruiting needs of other companies so they may readily need the services of independent recruiters.

Cold calling could be quite daunting initially, especially when you get lots of negative responses which is quite a common experience. The ability to look beyond the negative response is what makes a successful recruitment business. It's easy to get a list of businesses from the business directory and there are a few free online business directories that could be accessed easily, this directories always include phone numbers and email addresses, the key thing is to be able to access the manager who handles recruitment in the business, it's much easier to discuss with the decision maker. He or she will have the direct ability to involve you in accessing the company's vacancies.

It's very essential to be confident and professional over the phone, sometimes it might be easier to have a script written with what you want to say, this will help ease the initial nerves till you are able to handle the conversation with ease. It's essential to give yourself daily goals, you could pen down the amount of phone calls you want to make in a day and keep to it every day. Make it a vital habit and a part of your day, if you give yourself too large a goal you could find this daunting and tend to want to escape this part of your day, it's easier to set small targets each day initially, till you are able to have a build up of clients. Once you have a few vacancies to work on, the next big step is getting the right candidates to fill this role.

Many recruiters advertise vacancies across job boards for a fee, you might like to consider this option as well. Advertising on job boards opens up the vacancy to job seekers who are already interested in the vacancy and who might be well suited for the position as well. It is important to understand the role you are recruiting for, that way you will be able to take ownership of the role, it is also important to know exactly what the employer wants, from salary to location to past experience, not having the correct information on what the employer wants will result in you sending wrong CVs to the employer. Once the head-hunter is well informed on what the client's needs are with regards to the vacancies, it's easier to get the right candidates. There is nothing more irritating to clients than when they get loads of wrong and misplaced CVs. You could also do candidate searches on target CV database; you can purchase access to these CV databases for monthly fees or yearly fees depending on what the payment structure of the database is. Some databases are specialist database and only invite CVs that are particular to certain fields. Others are more general, and have loads of different CVs on them. This way you could easily search for the right candidates based on the qualities that the client is interested in.

Apart from databases, referrals are great ways to get fresh candidates, skin every CV that comes your way, don't be afraid to ask the candidates you talk to about their colleagues, candidates can generate other candidates for you through referral, they might know other candidates who are searching and who might have the skills you are looking for. A candidates CV will show his last place of work and they might need a replacement for him especially if he has already left this place of work, this method could provide fresh vacancies for you to work on.

Once you feel that you have the correct candidate, it's important to have a conversation with the candidate, you could easily talk with the candidate over the phone. It's important that the correct questions are asked, it's also very important that you allow the candidate to talk you through their experience and they should be able to tell you why they are right for the position. Many recruiters don't give the candidate a chance to talk, if you throw a vacancy at the candidate without proper questioning, the candidate would be misinformed and would either not turn up at interviews, or after the interview may turn down a job offer. Worse still they may stay on the job for a few weeks after which they find out that the job was never right for them in the first place and then make a run for it.

The most important part of a head-hunters job is securing the vacancy and sealing the deal, this is the perfect moment when the right candidate finds the right job and employer. It's hard work but it does pay off at the end of the day when the deal is finally sealed. The truth is that it's not always going to be easy and it might take a while to fill a vacancy sometimes. It may also take a lot of training and since the training is on the job, you will need a lot of hard work and consistency. Try to build a good client base by offering excellent customer service, and good candidates. Once a good client base is built and especially if you have offered excellent service in the past, the client will keep coming back to you with more vacancies for you to fill. You should however keep in touch with your clients because they will have more vacancies to fill from time to time. You need to be able to network with other head hunters as well, other head hunters might have vacancies while you have the right candidates, or they might have the right candidate while you have the vacancy to be filled. If you are able to network you will be able to work together with other head hunters in matching the candidates with right jobs while you split the fees with them once the deal is sealed. Some franchises give this sort of opportunities as a package, they give you access to a CV database and provide vacancies from companies as well as training and assistance for a fee. If you are going down the franchise route make sure that you get a good package. Some packages are better than others offering more support to you and your business. Read up more information in the section on franchises.

RESUME WRITING SERVICE

You can make money having a resume writing service, if you have a recruitment business already, this will enhance your business and you can get more clients for your resume writing business this way. You can build a website to suit this purpose, once your website has a high amount of traffic you can even monetise it by joining any of the affiliate or pay per click businesses already described above. You might be able to make money through it with Google ad sense, or any other affiliate program. A resume service allows you to use your experienced eye to help in building candidates CV's in the way that will attract other recruiters, you need to have some experience in knowing the best way to prepare a good CV. You need to know about using the right buzz words to create a great CV. Resume buzz words are very important in writing up an excellent CV, they are keywords that make CV's stand out. The CV must show the best skills that the candidates have to offer. You need to know how to prepare targeted resumes with skills and experience that are well suited for the right jobs, the targeted CV is excellent for when you have extensive skills and experience that targets the type of jobs you want. You also need to know how to prepare functional CVs; these types of CVs are excellent for entering the job market, or for when one is changing careers. They are used mostly when the candidates experience is not wide and extensive. Other types of CVs are the artistic types mostly used by graphic artist or people in advertising; it illustrates and showcases the work of the artists. You can also include cover letter writing as part of the package.

RUNNING YOUR EBAY BUSINESS

EBay is an auction site where items are listed and people bid for this items. You can make money from eBay in different ways, we have already mentioned how you can become an eBay affiliate, as an affiliate you don't have to sell anything to make money on eBay, what you need basically is your website or your blog and the link from eBay that lets your visitors link up to eBay from your site, when this visitors end up buying from eBay, you get commission.

Another way of making money on eBay is to actually sell on eBay. You need to create your sellers account with eBay to do this. You pay a small fee for every item you sell on bay. Many people have made some steady stream of income from eBay. It's easy to de-clutter your home and you will be surprised at what you can sell off on eBay. EBay is such a huge market online that you will get buyers looking for different items on there.

It's quite important that you build your profile first by getting some positive feedbacks first, you can do this by buying a lot of items first, and you can buy small items that you need on eBay so that over a period you get some positive ratings. Many eBay buyers will buy from people who have positive feedbacks only and if you have been able to build some positive feedbacks on your profile you get more customers bidding on your items readily.

You need to build a great listing which would attract your buyers. Since buyers search for products, the need to create a search engine friendly title cannot be over emphasised. Since eBay only allows searches from title and not description it's important that you get it right. You can do a search to find out how others are doing this with similar items, do not copy details as this would break the copyright law. When you want to do a search on similar items already sold just fill in the search box and check "completed items". This gives you an idea of what people are buying and how popular your type of product is. It's great to research what you want to list on eBay, you can watch similar items that people are bidding for as well and this will give you ideas on pricing.

Once you have the title right, you need to fill in the right description, it is important to accurately describe your item. Presentation is important in any type of business, and more importantly since your customers won't be seeing your items before purchase, the best way to give them a good idea of what you are selling is by accurately describing the product well. You also need to put on there a clear picture of the product. You should put in as much description as possible without falsifying any details. Falsifying details will not only get you negative feedback it might result into buyers taking action against you. You must avoid mistakes and grammatical errors in your descriptions as well as this may affect the value of your items. The turbo lister is also a great tool owned by eBay which allows you to upload bulk items for free, it allows you to create auctions offline, and upload by simply clicking the upload button.

Once you have accurately described your items you need to put the right pictures, make sure your picture correctly depicts the product, avoid background clutter, make sure picture is clear and sharp, this will help your buyers have a good idea of what your item looks like. EBay charges 12p for each extra shot but the first six shots are free; this will help you take multiple shots for expensive items. There is a way some ebayers have been able to upload free pictures on eBay as well, sites like photobucket or other photo hosting sites allow you to sign up with them, once you have signed up you upload your pictures where you are given a web address. Then add the photo on your eBay listing by clicking "add pictures", choose the "self hosting" tab and enter the web address where the pictures are hosted. This allows you to put pictures up for free.

Once your item is set for sale, you need to pick a start price for the bidding, its highly advised not to pick a high start of price, this might fend off potential buyers, lower start off prices attracts more bidders and the more bidders the higher the competition for your item. Higher competition will result in your item fetching a higher price at the end of bid than higher priced items. Low start of price also slashes the initial listing fee.

Most importantly you need to pick the right time, don't let your auction end time be in the middle of the night when the whole world is sleeping, or Monday mornings when people are up and about, ebayers have found out that evenings are best most especially Sunday evenings. Some items are seasonal and its best to target this periods with the seasonal items.

There are listing and closing fees to be paid with eBay. An auction type item which is under 99 pence and under is free, eBay sometimes allows listing fees for as low as 10 pence on some days which is quite great as this allows more money to be made on the item. Apart from a listing fee, there is also the closing fee; this is ten percent of the final sale price. Once you have started with making sales make sure you get proof of purchase as well as postal receipts and make sure you package your items properly, this gives it more value. The more payment options you give buyers, the more buyers you attract. PayPal is another option for payment for buyers, but sellers have to pay a fee and a percentage on the amount paid through pay pal, all these fees add up to the cost of the items, and these fees are quite compulsory as well.

You can bubble wrap the more delicate items or pack it with tissue this will prevent scratches on items or destruction of the items. A good tip is to try to deliver items on time this will give you positive feedbacks. Also remember that you might need to refund if items become broken or destroyed, so be ready in case this happens, also make sure you put the right postage price on your listing, all this will make your ratings increase positively. Make sure you look out for rogue buyers and bidders, and make sure you receive payment for item before shipping out.

The rules are slightly different for business traders, if you are a private seller you just sell off your things that you no longer need, but if you buy to resell you are a business trader and you are required to register as business sellers. Business sellers need to be more careful with description since all must be of satisfactory quality. Business sellers also have to refund an item if the buyer changes their mind within seven days of delivery. When buyers buy from business traders, they have rights which are the same as if they are buying from a shop. To be sure about your listing and closing fees as a business seller check eBay's fee chart for the correct fees you need to pay. If you become a business seller you need to bear in mind that you will need to pay your taxes. The most important tip is customer service; make sure you offer great customer service this will keep your customers coming back to you.

EBay Trade assistants

Another way to make a business from eBay is by becoming an eBay trade assistant, this means you are selling for others on eBay, selling as a trading assistant allows you to sell for others without having to find or buy the products yourself. You only need to list the items and watch the auction; you will need to ship out the items to the customers as well. Clients who don't have the time to sell themselves provide the items, and you are compensated for your efforts on the terms that you decide.

To become a Trading Assistant under EBay's standards, you need to have sold at least 4 times in the last 30 days, you should have a feedback score of 50 or higher, 97% or more of your feedback will be positive and your eBay account will be in good standing. Once you meet this standard, you can register to be a trading assistant, it's currently free to do this.

There is a lot of potential for business as a trade assistant, you are entitled to commissions on sale price of item, you need to think about how much commission you will earn and the program requires that you should agree with owner of item on the rate of commission, you might want the agreement in writing, this helps to resolve any disagreement after sale.

Highly priced items essentially mean bigger commission. One great method of achieving this is through B2B transactions, these sorts of transactions tend to involve higher value items, for success in this area you need to be on the lookout for persons or businesses selling. The good thing about this is low capital and a higher commission, you will be selling more expensive items and in larger amounts too, which is a win, win situation for you all the way.

STAYING AFLOAT

Eighty percent of business start-up collapses within the first two years, its one thing to start a business it's another thing to make a rolling success of one. I have learnt a few tips that will help your business stay alive.

TIME FACTOR: I have not yet seen a successful business man who does not value his or her time, time is what translates into money and it is a very precious weapon that you can use in combating failure. You need to concentrate your time on the things that grow your business even if they are things that you don't enjoy doing; you need to dedicate your precious time to these things. Time cannot be regained once it's lost and a failing business cannot afford to lose time by doing things that won't grow the business.

REALITY CHECK: If you are really struggling due to lack of expertise or lack of business know how you need to be able to ask for help quickly. Find a mentor who can talk you through how to get back on your feet. A mentor is someone who has been successful doing what you are trying to do and with lots of experience on how to break even in your business. Building a relationship with a mentor who is readily available to help you will help keep you grounded. If you can't find a business mentor then join an online community and business groups, don't try to go it alone you may not make it on the long run all alone, surround yourself with positive people.

BE FIRM: Your customers make your business survive, but it's no use if they don't pay up your invoices. Use your negotiating skills when it comes to getting your money paid, you might offer additional service or skills so your invoices are paid on time but be very quite firm. It's only fair that you get the reward for all jobs you have done. Watch out for customers who try to avoid payments, some financial instructions have packages that you can subscribe to for a fee, these packages allows you to check the credit rating of businesses so you know which businesses are in financial trouble before doing business with them, these packages also help you to send out debt recovery letters to any client found wanting.

CASH IS KING: Maintain a low overhead, don't spend money that you don't have or don't need, go for bargains, and watch out for ways you can cut cost, buy things wholesale if you use a lot of the product, keep cutting the cost of running your business as much as you can. The more you are able to lower your overhead the more your profits.

MARKETING TIPS: Effective marketing is needed for the survival of your business, it will bring in the business you need and open your business up to more customers. Telemarketing and cold calling can be a great method to generate sales for your business. Distributing fliers that market your products and services could be an effective way of advertising your business. Listing your business in free local business directory, yellow pages can also prove effective for you as well as listing in the local news paper. Don't undermine the power of 'word of mouth' referral as well. People talk to people and if you provide good services you will get referred. Write a small profile about your business on your email signature so that whenever you send emails you advertise your business. Keep marketing your business yourself, whenever you have the opportunity to talk about what you can offer don't pass it over, make sure you talk confidently about what you offer and sell your business constantly.

SKILL PROFILE

This is just a simple profile with questions to help you consciously and actively think of what type of skills you have and how your past experiences can be translated into a winning business. You can write down your skills and think of what business you can do with your skills. Remember that every skill you have is an asset. Your skills can easily translate into your business. We tend to put more effort into what we love doing most and we invest more time in what we love doing most, it's also great if we are able to identify what we love to do with our skills. Sometimes people have multiple skills this can create multiple streams of making money. I am a big advocate of multiple income streams since I have seen lots of situations where the only main streams of income coming into a home goes suddenly dry this instantly throws the whole family into a debacle. Think about how you can diversify your home business if you are already running one using the skills that you have or using new skills you have gained. The question in the profile list is not exhaustive, and it is meant to point you in the direction of your skill set and perhaps also point you in the direction of what you love doing most. This could help you establish a business. Many great businesses started small, and many started from a home office or a home's garage. It does not matter that you dream of owning a big conglomerate of firms nothing is unachievable even if you are only able to start small.

WHAT IS MY STRONGEST AMBITION?

- Think about it this way, apart from the money you get and the fulfilment you get from running your own business, your business should not really be about you, it should rather be about the people you are servicing with your products and services. It should be about meeting their needs or solving their problems through your product and services.
- What has being the driving force of your life and goals? What do you think drives people to become who they are? Read the biographies of people that you aspire to be like, people that your respect and who have managed to achieve the kinds of goals that you would dream of. What has been the driving force of their life? Underline what drives them and think about yourself what drives your life and the goals you will like to achieve?

- What figure of speech or analogy has been the best expression of your goals and ambition? If asked what best describes your goals and ambitions, what would you say? Would you say you are leading a dog's life? Do you think your life is over the hill? Or do you think life is like a ray of sunshine. This would help you realise what your attitude is to life and success. How you describe your life in a few words would point you to your fears and point you to the weaknesses and negative attitudes you need to work on to be able to achieve your dreams. If you think you are leading a dog's life, this would mean you think your goals and ambitions is not going in the direction you want, you can easily change this by taking up your skills to gradually building the type of business you want.
- If you suddenly realise your strongest ambitions are achievable, and your business goals can be actualised, how would you exploit and execute this information?
- What has stopped you in the past from moving in the direction of your strongest ambition?

YOU HAVE EXPERIENCES THAT CAN ENGINEER A SUCESSFUL BUSINESS

- How is achieving the blue print for your business and life's goal different from how other people operate and achieve theirs? What makes you different from others? What sets you apart from others and what skills do you possess that makes you unique? You can translate this into your business plans and propositions if you believe this uniqueness can translate into business success. Whatever makes you unique makes you do things your own way which is the best way you know how to. This can help you realise were you need help and where you might need more training before setting up the business you want.

- How the blue print for your life's goal is similar to the goal of the people that you admire and whose business goals you would love to emulate, what can you learn from other people's success?

- Write down something about the periods in your life when you have set goals for projects and failed to achieve the goal. What can you learn from it and how can you retrace your steps so that you don't duplicate the errors and failure

- What sort of things can you easily do, what are all the skills that you have ever acquired from past jobs and in your life generally, what can you easily do, is it writing, receiving phone calls, talking to people, surfing the internet, what special skills do you have, IT skills, typing skills? Graphics or arts? How can these translate into a business idea and plan?

- Do you feel irritated because the blueprint of your life is not going as planned?

- What are the things you will really like to do with your life?
- Do you have any fears about going it alone and starting up your own business?

YOU HAVE SKILLS THAT CAN BUILD AND ESTABLISH A SUCCESSFUL BUSINESS

- How have you lived your life daily, what are the daily activities that have made up your life in past years?
- What are the things that have stopped you from solving the kind of problems and rendering the kind of service that you really would want to?
- What will make it easier to be able to solve this type of problem and render this type of service to the people?
- What are the most common reasons people give for not starting a business, and how would you answer them?
- What could people do to kick start, plan and achieve the progress of their business? How would you make your own business a phenomenon in its niche?
- Is there someone you know that would pay money for the kind of service you can render and the kind of solutions you are willing to offer?

YOU HAVE ABILITIES THAT CAN CREATE A VIABLE BUSINESS

- What have you done in the past to make a success of any job you have worked at or how have you made a success of past assignment.
- What positive remarks have your colleagues, friends or family made about the way you handled jobs and assignments? What positive things does your former boss and colleagues and friends or family have to say about the way you carried out past assignments. What are the positives things you did in making past assignments a success?
- In past major projects, assignments and jobs you have done where have you struggled most? When have you had to stall or come to a standstill because of little or no progress?
- How has your past disappointments and failures pointed you in the right direction in past projects that you have done?
- What is most likely to be reasons to make you pack up a project, and what could you do to avoid this scenario or what solutions would you proffer to make you recoup in similar circumstances?

YOU HAVE SKILLS, ABILITIES AND EXPERIENCES THAT SERVE BUSINESS NEEDS, SOLVE PROBLEMS AND RENDER SOLUTIONS

- What type of assignments have you been able to easily put together and organise in the past?
- What do you love doing most that could be a service that translates into a business in your local community? What are you able to do to

meet a need that could bring money into your pocket?

- What skills have you gained from past projects, accomplishments and jobs that you could use to bring in money for yourself and your family while solving problems for others?
- How does comparing yourself with your colleagues in past positions or your friends and family made you realise the uniqueness of your skills? How does comparing yourself make you realise that you have different capabilities that you can bring into your own business?
- What business do you have the abilities to do based on your past experiences and skills you have used in the past?
- What can your business do to meet needs and to solve a problem or to render services to your community?

YOU CAN HAVE A SUCCESSFUL LONG TERM BUSINESS GOAL

- In a year's time where would you like your business to be and how do you plan to achieve this goal.
- What are some typical fears and cynical attitudes that people have about establishing the type of business you are proposing. What is keeping your form starting this business?
- What do you think is the best business that you can comfortably do; this might even become big business even if you have to start small?
- Write down how your skills can solve the problem of someone you know

- How do you think your business will survive compared to such businesses already in existence, how do you intent to make this business compete and survive in the market.
- How has this manual helped you in terms of starting your own small business from home? What are the best things that you think you have gained from the information given?
- Who has come to your mind that you can share your business idea with and how it can become a success?
- What is the next step you are going to take, what concrete step are you now going to take in starting you business and when are you going to write a business plan? See the sample business template and guide section in Appendices 1 and 2.

APPENDIX 1

NOTES/COMPENDIUM

Write down a sketch of your answers to the above questions; think about what you can do with all the positive experiences that you now realise that you have. Think about the business ideas that have been summarised in this manual in addition to any other ideas that you might have. Where do your skills, abilities and background fit in, use this as a basis of how you plan to make a success of your business and its modus operandi. If you like you can make this summary and notes a basis for your business plan. This answers that you give should help you build confidence in your capabilities and skills, and should help guide you in what steps you are able to make by yourself to build your business. I have a sample profile template below. Find a quiet corner and carefully answer each and every question stated above.

WHAT IS MY STRONGEST AMBITION?	
WHAT ARE YOUR EXPERIENCES THAT CAN ENGINEER A SUCCESSFUL BUSINESS?	
WHAT ARE YOUR SKILLS THAT CAN BUILD AND ESTABLISH A SUCCESSFUL BUSINESS?	
WHAT ARE YOUR ABILITIES THAT CAN CREATE A VIABLE BUSINESS?	

HOW CAN YOUR SKILLS, ABILITIES AND EXPERIENCES, SERVE BUSINESS NEEDS, SOLVE PROBLEMS AND RENDER SOLUTIONS?	
WHAT ARE YOUR SUCCESSFUL LONG TERM BUSINESS GOALS?	

APPENDIX 2

SAMPLE BUSINESS PLAN TEMPLATE

EXECUTIVE SUMMARY	
VISION –	
OBJECTIVES-	

PRESENT STATUS-	
INDUSTRY ANALYSIS – current situation only • The economy & business environment • The Market Place • Competition – who are they, what do they offer? • Market share – in each key market • E-commerce/ technology	
COMPANY ANALYSIS – current situation only • Your business –	

products and services – trends and description • Sales Template	
CUSTOMER ANALYSIS	
SWOT analysis • Relative strengths • Relative weaknesses • Opportunities • Threats	
Operation plan	

Marketing Strategies – your plan
 	
   • Marketing Mix (- product, place, pricing, promotion) – Target market
   • Positioning statement
   • Branding strategy
   • Product strategy
   • Pricing strategy
   • Distribution strategy
 	
   • Promotional strategy	

Sales forecast	

Resourcing requirements • The finance plan for your business plan • Investment from you? • The people involved	
Financial projections	
APPENDICES	

APPENDIX 3

SAMPLE BUSINESS PLAN GUIDELINE

This guideline is meant to help you understand how to answer the questions in the sample business template above.

Executive summary:

This might be about 3 to 5 pages; it is the summary of your business idea. The aim is to make your reader more interested in the whole document, and it's like a flavour of what is to come in the main body of your business plan.

Vision:

In this section describe what your vision is for your business. What do you want to be? Describe where your business will be in five years time.

Objectives:

Explain your long term values in setting up and expanding your business. What are your values? Is it to get rich, to build a big business, and create employment for yourself and others?

Present status:

Where are you now? What is your background and progress to date?

Industry analysis

This section describes the market where your company will be competing and where it will operate, this section will give answers to well researched market research questions, it will examine the technologies currently in place and its trends and developments and how you will respond to this.

This section also identifies who the company's competitors are, and the strengths and weaknesses of these competitors. It shows what competitive edge the company has over its competitors. You will detail the market share of your products, trends, market trends, user customer profile, market size

Company analysis

This section gives a detailed overview of what your company offers, it gives the details of the company's product and services, it gives the size of company, it also details what the unique qualification your company has in serving its target market. Describe how your company fulfils a real need in such a way that the benefits are attractive to customers and users, and how you can effectively and easily communicate your unique serving point to end users.

Customer analysis

This section analyzes the customer segment that your business serves. The segment also analyzes and conveys the needs of the customers; it also gives a detailed report of why the customers will pay for the company's product. Show how your business will meet the needs of the customers. Review customers buying habits.

Discuss price, quality, and promotional distribution from customer's point of view; discuss how competitor's products are positioned from customer's point of view.

SWOT analysis

SWOT analysis is the subjective analysis of data that helps the understanding, presentation, discussion and decision-making in the business, it sheds lights on the pros and cons of the business, the strength and weaknesses of your business. It also sheds more light on the opportunities your business can take advantage of in the market place and the threats your business faces as well.

STRENGHTS could be your specialist marketing expertise, a new, innovative product or service. It could be any aspects of your business that adds value to your product and service.

WEAKNESSES: This could be a lack of marketing expertise, location of your business or poor quality goods or services, damaged reputation.

OPPORTUNITIES: Your business opportunities could be a developing market such as the Internet. It could be your competitor's vulnerability, Niche target markets, Business and product development, Seasonal, weather, fashion influences or better technology.

THREATS: This could be a new competitor in your home market or price wars with competitors. A threat could be that a competitor has a new, innovative product or service. Threats could also be competitors that have superior access to channels of distribution; it could also be the recession or a poor economy. It could be any other obstacles faced by your business in the market place.

Operation plan

This section gives concise details about where you are going and how you are going to get there. It gives a detailed plan on what's involved in running the business. How you are going to make a success of your home based business, equipment needs, are laid out here in black and white. Your operating cost projections, your operating methods and procedures are all detailed in this section.

Marketing strategy / sales forecast

This section detail exactly what steps will be taken to ensure that customers know about your product/service and prefer it over the competition. Even though you are planning to run a home business you need a marketing strategy and its needs to be well detailed. You will have a positioning statement; this is a strong statement that shows how your company will be perceived in the mind of your target market. You need to detail your strategy in relation to functional areas- product, place, pricing, promotion, technology, operations. How will you establish your brand? What methods will you be using to promote and distribute your products? What are your cash flow projections and what is your sales forecast?

Resourcing requirements

This section gives details on how your business will be financed, will you be getting a loan and who will be loaning you the money? How do you plan to repay?

Financial projections

Projected profit and loss, cash flows and projected balance sheet, input your projections sales and costs based on your previous research. Introduce projected income statement (profit & loss account) Give monthly cash flow projection for the first year. Give a projected balance sheet, if the business is pure starts up then opening balance will be zero. The balance sheet is also known as your businesses financial position; it's a statement that shows what your company owns and what it owes at a particular time.

Appendices

Includes tables and graphs explaining size of market, segmentation, competition, market shares, growth patterns, distribution channels, price/quality segments, customer categories, future trends, market share/segmentation projections etc. Summarize your main findings in the markets section within the body of your plan.

It also includes all necessary extras like promotional materials, product photos, and independent assessments

RESOURCES TO AID YOUR RESEARCH

www.home-based-businesses-resource.com

http://en.wikipedia.org

www.sba.gov

www.arise.com

www.alpineaccess.com

www.abta.com

http://agentcommunity.liveops.com

www.ossn.com

www.freedomtravelgroup.co.uk

www.futuretravelcareers.co.uk

www.ebay.com

www.petgroomer.com

www.nationaldoggroomers.com

ABOUT THE AUTHOR

Joanna Akins is a home based business woman, a mum and a lovely wife.

She has a first degree in microbiology and holds a master's degree in plant biotechnology. She formerly worked as an application specialist before leaving her day job to look after her kids and family. She loves to write and also now runs her own home based businesses happily juggling these with her home life.